Excuse Me, I'm in 2A:
Conversations at 35,000 Feet

by
K. J. Cauthen

Copyright © 2013 K. J. Cauthen
All rights reserved.
ISBN-10: 0615625339
EAN-13: 9780615625331

To my children

You have been my inspiration and purpose as I have traveled along life's wonderful and sometimes difficult path. I only hope I have inspired you and been a positive role model. Remember— you only get one chance to make a first impression.

CONTENTS

Introduction IX
Chapter One – The Relater Experience 1
Chapter Two – Our Youth Are Our Future 5
Chapter Three – The Diva 11
Chapter Four – The Angry Plane 17
Chapter Five – Are You Stuck? 23
Chapter Six – We All Know Someone 27
Chapter Seven – Color Blind 31
Chapter Eight – Dr. Ken 37
Chapter Nine – He Has a Secret 41
Chapter Ten – We Are Just Procrastinators 45
Chapter Eleven – What's Your Occupation? 49
Chapter Twelve – The Crazy Things People
                Do and Wear on a Flight or in an Airport 53
Chapter Thirteen – The Crying Child 57
Chapter Fourteen – Honey, Put the Seat Down 61
Chapter Fifteen – Expectations 65
Chapter Sixteen – Where Are You From? 71
Chapter Seventeen – I Love Music 75
Chapter Eighteen – I Am Proud to Have Served 77
Chapter Nineteen – There Is a Time and a Season for Everything . . . 83

Acknowledgments 89
Thank You 91
About the Author 93

Excuse Me, I'm in 2A

K. J. Cauthen

INTRODUCTION

You are about to read a collection of personal stories based on conversations I have had during my many years of traveling the skyways at 35,000 feet. I am using 2C as an example, for uniformity purposes, as I could have been in 3D or 29C. If you are a frequent flyer, many of my accounts of conversations with fellow passengers and personal stories will surely ring a tone of familiarity. You may almost feel like you were there beside me in 2A. Hey, maybe you were, and one of the stories is about you. Anyway, if not, I think you will get a good dose of my life's lessons, my personal accounts, and your doctor's recommended shot of laughter from my encounters with normal folks like you and some not so normal, as you will soon see.

I first got this idea to write about my travels a few years ago, while I was having a conversation with a fellow traveler. We were on a two-hour flight, having a good ole time, and I said to her, "The things we say and share on a two-hour flight." I told her that perhaps the reason we share so much with complete strangers at 35,000 feet is because It seems private. When it's just you, God, and a total stranger, you feel like you can be more honest. A conversational remark, such as, "How are you doing today?" Somehow turns out to be a two-hour heart-to-heart conversation with a person who is slowly becoming your "BFF."

Occasionally flights end up with what I call "conversation overflows." Sometimes a loud person, who must not be aware of how well his voice carries, really opens up with a newfound friend just a few seats ahead of you. You think to yourself, if you were the Internal Revenue Service, you would have enough to open an investigation, as he is up there divulging his every last secret to a complete stranger. You know the ones I'm talking about. Then you and your seatmate in 2A look at each other and make a joke, which starts a conversation about the loudmouth pair up ahead, and there you go again. You too begin your own tell-all. Sound familiar?

There are a few folks that try to do the "I'm busy and important, so don't talk to me" thing. They type away on their laptop or read and edit the documents they wrote for a big meeting. I must admit, after a few of the lengthy tell-all I have endured, I have started to use some of their tactics. I do like some "me" time, and sometimes I simply want to get to where I'm going quietly. Hey, I'm not Dr. Phil. Though, you will soon see that I have felt like I needed to be on more than one occasion.

One tactic I have tried to use to avoid the soon-to-be-new friend is to immediately place my headphones on my ears and pretend to be listening to music. Though I am somewhat of a worrier, and it would drive me crazy to miss any announcements from the flight attendant, so I usually don't have the music going and only pretend to be listening.

Sometimes I take out *USA Today* and try to read without interruption. Of course, there is often going to be an individual so in need of a friend who interrupts me by asking, "What's going on today?" I want to say, "Oh, just someone trying to mind their own business." But I choose the more friendly path and say, "Oh, nothing much, just the folks in Washington messing everything up as usual," or whatever the headline is for that day. And there I am again—on a new adventure into someone else's life, about to learn everything about this person that just five minutes earlier I thought I didn't want to know.

As I began to write down my stories, I found myself doing some soul-searching and rethinking of situations that I really didn't expect. It has been a journey back in time, and I have discovered and reflected on many things in my life and the opinions I have as I worked on the book. One thing I noticed, which I'm sure you will see immediately, is the tremendous influence my mother, Gladys, has had and continues to have

INTRODUCTION

in my life. Some stories produced tears, as they really touched my heart and brought back old memories. For the most part, however, the stories made me think and ask questions. I have also felt my spirits lifted with hope, inspiration, and laughter from reliving some truly interesting and often funny moments during my travels.

I hope my stories have the same influence on you. If nothing else, I hope my stories take you away from your busy schedule of travel, work, school, or preparing the family dinner and offer you a moment of light-hearted pleasure.

Hey, if you don't find enjoyment in the stories, it's not my fault; you should have sat next to me in 2A. I can only say that I'm glad I listened to the person in 2A more than to my "music."

Enjoy!

CHAPTER ONE

THE RELATER EXPERIENCE

It seems that on a two-hour flight, there is often a person next to you that you just click with. It feels as though you understand and can relate to each other. It's as if you have known this person your entire life. Maybe the way you grew up is similar, or you are currently experiencing the same problems in your lives. Bottom line, in those two hours, you bond. Perhaps you think, "Gee, why can't I get along this well with my significant other?" You might wonder later, "Why did I relate so well with this person during my flight?"

That's it…it's a two-hour flight. Get it? Life in real time is not a quick snapshot; it's the whole tamale. And tell me really, when was the last time you listened to someone related to you without interruption for two hours? I would imagine it's been a long time—maybe never. We are all so busy, and we have way too many distractions. We seem to lose contact and lose the relationships with the ones we love the most or those special friends. I know that when my friends call, I'm usually trying to do one hundred different things, and I find that I rarely really listen to them. Sometimes I've even forgotten whom I was talking to on the phone, and I don't even remember what we were talking about just seconds after I hang up. I'm sure you have done the same thing.

So when you find yourself sharing intimately with someone at 35,000 feet, just realize that you really are not relating to this person any better than you could or would with anybody else in your life. You are just trapped, and you are finally *listening*!

Here is a story for you.

On a flight to Columbia, South Carolina, I had a "relater experience." We talked about everything, as we seemed to have similar interests. I had noticed that she was a little overweight for her height and body frame, but I decided not to say anything about it. I must admit I tried the earphones trick at first, but she was good and had me talking less than fifteen minutes into the flight.

We started out talking about her kids, which were similar ages to my younger kids. We talked about our kids' schools, and I told her about a wonderful free online learning tool called "Khan Academy." I highly recommended the website to her because I've found it to be very good.

The lady started bragging about how her kids were doing very well in school and how proud she was of them. I then chimed in and told her that their accomplishments were not by accident, as it takes parents and guardians to guide their kids to want to achieve. She agreed. We then discussed the challenges our kids face today and how far technology has come. We reminisced about those ten-pound-brick mobile phones. Cell phones were so big that they had to be carried, with their eight-pound batteries, in a large bag with a shoulder strap. We each felt like cell phones have changed a lot in a short amount of time.

We laughed at how smart kids are today. I told her my eighth grader was learning things that I learned in high school. I remarked that I thought it was truly amazing that reports keep ranking America behind other countries in education.

An article in USA Today dated 10 December, 2010 from The Associated Press stated that: *"United States students are continuing to trail behind their peers in a pack of higher performing nations, according to results from a key international assessment. Scores from the 2009 Program for International Student Assessment showed 15-year-old students in the U.S. performing about average in reading and science, and below average in math. Out of 34 countries, the U.S. ranked 14th in reading, 17th in science and 25th in math. Those scores are all higher than those from 2003 and 2006, but far behind the highest scoring countries, which includes South Korea, Finland, Singapore, Hong Kong and Shanghai in China and Canada.*

"*Between 1995 and 2008, for example, the United States slipped from ranking second in college graduation rates to 13th, according to the Organization for Economic Co-operation and Development, the Paris-based organization that develops and administers the PISA exam. Of 34 OECD countries, only 8 have a lower high school graduation rate.*

"*Responding to the grim figures, President Obama has set a goal for the U.S. to have the highest proportion of students graduating from college in 2020.*"

During our conversation I wondered what the American ranking was when I was a kid. Growing up, I thought I was being challenged pretty hard. Were our standards lower then? Are today's kids being challenged earlier? I told her that I bet the kids in China are probably learning algebra in kindergarten.

Next thing I knew I was telling her my childhood experience and that my father was not an involved parent. He liked to be alone and probably drank a little too much alcohol. He seemed just fine going to work every day and minding his own business, and we kids knew to do the same. I told her that as a child I couldn't remember him ever telling me to do anything. As I got older, though, he actually helped me make a big career decision.

My frustration by my father's lack of support and attention to his family has always pushed me to be a very actively engaged father; my younger daughter would maybe say I'm too engaged. I feel, however, that I have made mistakes along the way trying to figure out just how to parent, as I didn't have a good role model. I often make adjustments to my actions and reactions, as I want my kids to look to me as a role model when they become parents.

I told her that I sometimes wonder what my dad thought all the fuss was about during the third Sunday in June, otherwise known as Father's Day. She let out a big laugh and told me I was very funny.

Then, to my surprise, my new friend brought up the topic that she needed to lose weight. I had never known a woman to bring that subject up out of the blue. I would never dare to bring it up on my own. I suggested Weight Watchers to her, as several of my friends had success with this program; she agreed and said that she was going to look into it.

I thought for a minute and told her that if I were to suggest my wife look into Weight Watchers, she would likely be offended and assume I had a problem with her weight. For the record, I do not. She looks great, especially after giving birth to two beautiful children. I told the lady that it was very important that she recognized her issue with weight and it was time for her to do something about it. She said that she has had a problem for some time, but had chosen to ignore it and do nothing. I told her it was more than her appearance; losing weight was important for her health.

A two-hour flight with nowhere to go and nothing to do but discuss our issues gives us the courage to talk about things we normally wouldn't, and the fact that we will probably never see each other again helps. I think in the end, the conversation between the lady and me helped us both, as I had not discussed my dad's lack of commitment and support to anyone other than family.

I hope that through our conversation she will finally gain the confidence to do something about her weight. The conversation we had could be a life-changing and lifesaving experience. Let's all hope she followed through on her decision to do something about her weight, as obesity is definitely a huge health issue in America. If you are experiencing similar problems with your weight, I have two things for you to do: talk to your doctor and get moving.

I'm glad I was there for her in 2C.

CHAPTER TWO

OUR YOUTH ARE OUR FUTURE

A few years ago I had the pleasure of sitting beside a wonderful, confident eighteen-year-old girl. We started out simply talking about why we were traveling, and she mentioned that she had been visiting her aunt and was returning home to start college. I told her it was great that she was starting college and that her parents must be proud. She said yes and then revealed that her parents were divorced. She explained that she never used her situation as an excuse, but as a reason to pursue her dreams. As I listened to her, I thought she sounded like a very courageous young lady, and we continued our conversation.

As we discussed her future plans and her turbulent times with her dad, I noticed that she was very mature for her age, and she looked older than eighteen. I guess the flight attendant thought the same, as she kept asking her if she would care for a glass of wine. She politely said no each time, and we joked about the fact that the attendant would be embarrassed if she knew her age. I told her that maybe the flight attendant was like me: the older I get, the younger everyone looks. It is getting harder to tell a forty-year-old mom from her eighteen-year-old daughter as they walk down the street, especially with the words "Juicy" and "Pink" on the back of their shorts. We shared a big laugh on that one. She seemed to be a very conservative young lady who would not wear "Pink" on the back of her shorts. For the record, I'm not a big fan of that attire. But I know that folks who wear that type of clothing are just being themselves, and there is nothing wrong with that.

She went on to tell me that she never drank alcohol or smoked, which she credited in part to the rough life she had with her dad being an alcoholic and addicted to drugs. I learned that her parents divorced when she was six and she had to go back and forth between the two of them for a long time. Finally she was old enough to say that she didn't care to be around her dad. And she told me that she had not seen him in many years.

This young woman on the plane beside me didn't realize it, but I had been in a similar situation with my older kids. At one point in my life, I had not seen them for what seemed like an eternity. We later reestablished a nice relationship. But then things turned sour again, and we have not communicated for some time now. Anyone who has lost contact with a family member knows that you can't get back the lost time. I consider myself a good father, and I regret that my older kids' mom and I divorced, but that's life. There is obviously some resentment and unanswered issues that are hard for my older kids to handle.

I would say to any young adults who are going through a similar situation that parents' lives and past are their own, and children should love their parents for the individuals they are. I had to learn that myself, and I'm truly grateful I did before it was too late.

She told me that her dad was an example to her of what dependency on alcohol and drugs looks like and what it can do to your life, so she would never do drugs. I asked her how she handled the stress of peer pressure to try drugs and alcohol.

What she said next somewhat changed my view of how she was dealing with her situation. She said that she had decided a long time ago that she knew what she wanted out of life and she had to get it for herself. She said she didn't have a dad to support her, even though her mother later remarried. The divorce and her dad's addictions made her feel like she had to depend on herself alone because other people would let her down and not be there for her. I felt sad for her, as I suddenly realized I was listening to a really sad little girl that was trying to be strong.

Hearing her story showed me the negative effects divorce and addictions have on families. I also learned the important roles both parents play in children's lives, divorced or not. This young lady had a loving mother and, from what I had heard, a caring stepfather. Yet she was still hurt by the actions and lack of love and support from her biological father.

I told her that she needed to look at her mother, who had cared for her, and the role her stepfather had played in her life, as proof that she could trust people. I encouraged her to realize that the people in her life had been there for her. I told her that I have learned to accept that people make mistakes and sometimes their mistakes affect others, as her parents' divorce had obviously been a terrible experience for her. I also urged her to try to find a way to accept her dad's addictions as an illness. I said that I felt she was right to distance herself from him during this time. But I told her it would be important, after some time had passed, for her focus on understanding the illness that surrounds alcoholism and drug addiction instead of focusing on her father's absence from her life.

I mentioned to her that hopefully someday her dad would get well. I said I hoped she would get an opportunity to have a relationship with her real dad and replace the memories of his addictive behavior with new memories. But I said she would have to be willing to be open to this if the opportunity came.

I then mentioned my dad's use of alcohol and his lack of family support. I told her how I never sent him a Father's Day cards until I realized that, regardless of the choices he made in his life, he was still my father. I began to send him Father's Day cards and tried to see him in a different light, as much time had passed and he was much older. I told her that I'm glad that before he passed away in 2002 we had established a pretty good relationship. He actually gave me great advice to retire from the military. Prior to my conversation with him, I had been struggling with the decision of whether to retire. But he put it to me in common-sense terms: It is a very complicated decision to let go and change from something you love and have been doing for twenty years or more.

I later retired and found a new job. If I had not retired when I did, I would have missed the opportunity. Therefore I always give my dad credit for helping me make one of the biggest and better decisions of my life.

But my willingness to forgive and accept him gave us that opportunity, and it now allows me to have a great memory of my dad. I told her that later in life I also realized that much of my view of my dad was based on my mother's statements about him to me. When I allowed myself to get away from viewing my dad through my mother's eyes, I could not see all the negatives she had spoken of throughout my younger years. I'm sure she had good enough reasons to talk badly of him, but as his son, I am glad I matured and started to see my father through my own eyes. Now, being married myself, I know my wife is still hot about things I did ten years ago. And I swear I don't remember any of those things, but she will never let me forget.

The young lady said she got my point. She said she would be willing to keep an open mind and look at her father through her own eyes.

I was hoping my advice to her didn't seem too much like a lecture, and I began to notice her looking around and acting as if she had never flown in first class. I asked her about whether this was her first time, and she said that her aunt had upgraded her ticket to first class and she was enjoying the perks. She took out her camera and was about to take a picture. I then offered to take a picture of her, and she gave me a big smile. Later in the flight, the camera came out again as she was eating the meal that the attendant had delivered. I took another picture for her to remember the experience of her first time flying first class; I had a feeling that it wouldn't be this young lady's last time.

She told me that she was an "A" student and had gotten a scholarship to attend a local community college because of her academic performance in high school. But she wanted to go to a four-year school and experience the full college environment and live on campus. I told her that, from my perspective of having two adult children from a previous relationship, I understood how tough it was to deal with divorce. I told her it was admirable that despite what some would say was a bad situation she had gathered strength to stay positive and do great in school.

She then told me she had actually gone on a campus tour of a school while visiting her aunt, but her stepdad immediately started putting the negative spin on her activities. She asked me, "Why do grown-ups do that?" I told her that it's going to be hard for me to allow my younger children to go away to college as well, as I still see my adult children as if they are only twelve years old and not the mature young adults they have become. I started laughing as I remembered my sixth-grade daughter and I had recently seen the movie *College Road Trip*, starring Martin Lawrence. We loved that movie. My daughter says that I'm exactly like the daddy character in the movie—very protective.

The young lady in 2A really made an impact on me and made me reflect on my life's situations. Her mother, stepdad, and father should be very proud. I hope she gets the chance to attend a four-year college program and live on campus in the dorms as she mentioned. I really enjoyed my conversation with the young lady and seeing how mature she was at the age of eighteen will probably benefit my daughter as she tries to convince me of how mature she is when it's time for her to go off to school; however, for now I will remain more like the daddy character in *College Road Trip*.

CHAPTER THREE

THE DIVA

By this point you may be seeing a trend that many of my stories involve conversations with women. My wife pointed that out to me when I first started writing this book. But you will see—I do have stories that involve men in 2A.

I admit that I have always had the gift of easy conversation with both men and women. My family points out that everyone wants to tell me their stories and acts as if they have known me forever only a few minutes after meeting me. This "gift," some might call it, though, has given me more than its share of problems.

Once, my family and I were on vacation in Fort Lauderdale, Florida. We were enjoying the beautiful pool area at the hotel. I decided to take a little break and headed over to the Jacuzzi for a little relaxation while my wife watched our seven- and three-year-old kids. I had been eying it for a while, and there wasn't anyone else using it, so I settled myself in for a nice, relaxing dip.

Within no time at all, my private and relaxing Jacuzzi suddenly became the happening spot. Four ladies in their forties had arrived. They looked like they had come down to Florida for a little girl-time. They were all dressed up in their new bikinis, and their deep tans made them look like they had been there for at least a week.

We started talking about different topics: the beautiful property, our families, and suggestions of where to go eat later. We were just having a good ole time. I looked over at my wife, who was a couple of yards away, and pointed her out to my new friends. I motioned for her to come over and meet the girls.

I guess the laughter got a little much, and soon the messenger, my seven-year-old daughter, delivered it straight over like the Pony Express. Right in front of everyone, she announced, "Daddy, Mommy said you need to stop talking to these women and get out of the pool now." This, of course, caused a quick pause in the laughter, and I excused myself from my new friends. I eased my way out of the Jacuzzi and started the damage control.

We later saw the group of ladies, and they were pointing me out and laughing. My wife, smarty-pants as she can be sometimes, said, "A little Jacuzzi time later." I replied, "Yes, maybe later, much later." I never did indulge again on that trip, of course. To this day, I still have a quick recall of that situation, which brings a smile to my face every time I get into a Jacuzzi.

This is just one example of how I have always found that people love to talk to me. And I must say I open up and share easily with others about similar situations or problems. I guess I'm just a good relater.

So here is a good one. Every time I remember this story, I still can't believe it happened. This particular story is…OK, it's funny, but it actually happened. I call it "The Diva."

This day I was traveling to New York City, The Big Apple. My sister lived in Long Island, and I was flying to visit her there. I arrived at my seat to find a very attractive lady in her early thirties with blonde hair. She was wearing a low-cut top, and the rest of her clothing did not hold anything back from the imagination. She was holding a very expensive-looking fur coat and a small doggie kennel—the kind Paris Hilton would carry. I could tell immediately that she was *someone*; she was obviously used to the finer things in life. As I was settling into my seat, she immediately told me she needed a drink because she had had an extremely rough morning.

THE DIVA

When we landed, I told my new friend not to give her dog to a complete stranger again and to take care. She said, "I didn't. You are my friend, right?" I said, "Yes, I guess I am." She paraded off the plane, and I was left with a story that my wife and I still laugh about to this day.

CHAPTER FOUR

THE ANGRY PLANE

There is, in my opinion, no other setting with the same potential for crazy situations than an airplane. Often the crew members have been flying all day or for a few days and are probably trying to get home to take care of their own different life situations. And the passengers have been told lie after lie about what time their flight is arriving and departing. These people are flying for hundreds of different reasons and are often stressed out. Add a few crying babies, barking dogs, and alcohol to the mix…and you have a real "angry plane" flying at 35,000 feet.

If you are a frequent flyer, you are probably like me and have seen more than your share of angry-plane situations.

For the most part, if you are a frequent business traveler, you are able to fly first class, as is my situation. And I live for the perks of reward membership, but occasionally it doesn't work out and I get to experience fun in coach.

On one occasion, I was seated in the middle of the plane, and a fairly nice-looking young man entered with a dog carrier. He was in his thirties and looked like he had all of his marbles, but soon we all would learn he had a few issues. The flight attendant came over and advised him to place the carrier under the seat and to also close the bag, as the dog could not be out. The young man snapped at the flight attendant and said, "My baby needs to breathe. He is fine. Move along." The flight attendant was very cool in his demeanor and walked away. A few moments later he returned and again asked the man to place the dog in the carrier and under the seat. The plane at this time was actually moving away from the gate and headed for the runway. This time the passenger was even more aggressively raised his voice and told the flight attendant that his dog would suffocate if he placed him in the carrier, and he yelled to the flight attendant to leave him and his dog the hell alone.

As the flight attendant was leaving, the passenger called him an "asshole." I was impressed by the attendant's reaction, as he kept his cool and walked to the front of the plane. I thought he was going to take the abuse of the passenger and let him have his way, until the plane made a sudden right-turn off the runway...and we headed back to the terminal. Everyone in the immediate area started commenting to the passenger. One lady really gave him her piece of mind, saying, "I hope you are happy now. You are going to make us all suffer for your stupidity." He tried to change his tune and was yelling for the attendant that he was sorry, without success. As we arrived back at the terminal, the captain came out and told him to get off his airplane. Everyone started clapping and saying good-bye in not-so-nice words, as we would now be forty minutes delayed.

On another flight, I found myself in 15C with two passengers seated next to me; it turns out they were husband and wife returning home from visiting family. Now, you know how stressful get-togethers with relations can be.

We sat down as we boarded and exchanged a quick hello and a smile. I had the aisle seat, the husband was at the window seat, and the wife was seated in the middle. They both seemed pleasant and both made a few comments, and then we all went on to our private affairs.

Later in the flight, the wife asked me how much longer until the plane lands, and I told her what I thought was the answer. Then we started a little small talk. The husband was right there next to her and was listening to every word. She described their family, and I told her my family situation and that I lived in Florida. She described their trip had been, and we laughed because I shared with her that I know visiting family can be stressful. Then, without warning, her husband looked at her and angrily said, "Are you going to flirt with that man with me sitting right here?" He called her a few bad words and then looked at me.

I was shocked, as he had been right next to her listening to the conversation, and she and I were just talking about family stuff and passing the time. He had even, and at first I didn't know how to respond. Finally I said, "Sir, I want to say I'm sorry for speaking to your wife, as it has obviously bothered you." I also told him that I thought he was also part of the conversation. She was noticeably embarrassed and knew that our conversation was not inappropriate.

I felt so bad for this lady and wonder what type of daily hell this guy puts her through. I felt that his behavior was definitely abusive, as she simply sat there and took his comments and belittlement. She remained quiet for the remainder of the flight.

I sat there in silence as well, thinking how sorry I was for this lady. Of course, I wanted to say something more. But I thought it best to let it go, not knowing what this crazy guy was capable of doing.

I guess this is the message: Abuse can be something that starts out as belittlement, mental abuse, or physical abuse. Those around you might see it but feel helpless and not be in a situation to help you.

You need to be strong and help yourself…

Sometimes the plane is not angry, but you find yourself by a person with a gift they insist on sharing with you. I found myself in this situation seated next to a lady that seemed to be very happy and was very colorful. The shades of her clothing came from every color in a crayon box. We started some light conversation, and she asked what I did for work. I told her that I do some consulting and had retired from the military. I then asked her what she did, and it all came together. She said that she was a fortuneteller and wrote a column in a few major newspapers. I was very surprised and she immediately wanted me to give her my palm so she could "do a reading." I told her, "No, I am fine to just let time play itself out and not know ahead of time what's was going to happen." She started laughing and said that usually when people learned who she was, they begged her to tell them their future.

She started asking me about my life, which she said was interesting. And I found her to be very interesting as well. I asked her how she had gotten into her line of work, and she said that she always had very specific feelings about people when she met them for the first time, and she could tell things about their lives that she had no way of knowing. She seemed to really believe she had "the gift," as the famous "Ms. Cleo" would say. Ms. Cleo was a famous fortuneteller on television that later got caught up in a scandal.

I admitted to the fortuneteller that I thought all that stuff was a scam and didn't believe in it myself. She then closed her eyes and said, "Wait a minute…I see…I see…" I said, "Stop…Hey, no…no…no readings. OK, I believe you. You are a great fortune teller." She started laughing and told me quickly that she saw goodness in me—and happiness. I said, "OK…that's good…"

We continued with some light conversation. The plane landed and we said good-bye.

Now, to show that the situations I find myself in on flights is not always crazy…I was back in 2C again, and a man placed a gentle touch on my shoulder to get my attention. An elderly man, very soft-spoken, stated to me, "Young man, would you do me a favor and switch seats with me? That is my wife next to you." I of course said that I would love to, which was a little lie, as he was in a front seat: 1C. This seat location required passengers to place their laptop bag or small personal bags in the overhead compartment, which was a little hassle. But, hey, he wanted to sit with his bride, so we switched seats.

During the flight I overheard and witnessed the husband and wife, who had to be in their late seventies or early eighties engage in a ritual of mutual respect and care for one another. He helped her, and she helped him with everything from wiping a piece of food from his mouth to asking him if he needed the reading light. They conversed easily and seemed to be having a wonderful flight together.

It was a pleasure to witness two people in love at such an elderly age. I thought about how wonderful it would be to be blessed to live as long as they had as loving partners.

Once we landed, the elderly gentlemen stood and handed me a business card. On it he had written with his unstable hand, "Thank you very much for changing seats with my wife and me. We are celebrating our sixtieth wedding anniversary." He told me he had recently retired from his position and they were taking a vacation. The front of the card had his title; he had recently retired as the president of a prestigious all-black college.

Their exchange and display of love and affection touched me so much that I called my wife as soon as I could and told her I missed her and loved her. She of course asked me what I had done wrong. I told her about the couple. My wife agreed that it was a nice story, and she was glad I shared it with her. She thanked me for the call.

I am glad I was there to help them sit together and to witness their love.

CHAPTER FIVE

ARE YOU STUCK?

Many of my conversations through the years with men onboard flights at 35,000 feet have been about family and work. Especially work. Men, it seems, are defined by their work. If I have learned anything over the years, it is that family and love of others is what completes me. It gives me purpose to give of myself to those I love without needing anything in return. Women, it seems, instinctively know this almost from birth. I find, however, that few men ever get it. Men feel that they need to control something. They need to have a title to be worthy of love and honor. Those who know me know that my most precious title is "Dad." I've worked hard to earn that title and the respect and honor that go with it every day.

Most of my life has been grounded by my relationships with two people. One is definitely my mother, Gladys, and the other is my relationship with Christ. I'll just leave the religion aspect alone for now and continue about my mother. She had a saying for almost everything. And in my opinion, she was one of the smartest people I have ever known. She passed away in 2001, but she still lives on in my memories and stories.

One of my mother's sayings came up when people got themselves in a jam, such as the incident and media craze over Congressman Weiner. He got in trouble for sending texts and pictures of himself to a young lady who was not his wife. He made up the excuse that someone had hacked his computer. He later admitted his guilt to the news media and his pregnant wife. Gladys would say of that situation, "You are stuck now." We as children translated her statement to mean: you made a mistake, you are in a jam, or you simply screwed up. We can relate to the congressman and say, "He definitely got himself stuck."

Many of the conversations I have had at 35,000 feet have been with folks who are having a run of bad luck with work or family. And my response always revolves around the Gladys phenomenon of "being stuck," and discussions of how to get "unstuck."

One of my brothers, God rest his soul, served in Vietnam, with the Eighty-Second Airborne Division. He returned as many of our brave and courageous veterans do, a little shaken mentally. In those days the military didn't support or recognize the mental wounds that war had on our military personnel. These mental problems were often left for family members to discover and cope with. The military and private support groups, to their credit, are starting to do a better job today. One great example is the "Wounded Warrior Project." My brother finally learned to deal with his time spent in war and led a pretty normal life; he died from complications of cancer in 2008.

It was tough going when he first got home. He normally didn't talk about his time in Vietnam, but he would talk to me about it from time to time.

During one of our talks, he described a flying mission in which he parachuted into a hot landing zone. He said that he could hear the bullets passing by his ears as the enemy shot at him and his fellow airborne soldiers. He said that he looked to his left and right while he was coming down and he could see men slumped over, already dead from bullet wounds. When he landed on the ground, it was chaos. Men were running in all directions to get out of harm's way and organizer themselves so they could carry out the mission. He said something just told him to stay put. And when he hit the ground, he stood still for what seemed like an eternity. Then something told him it was safe to move on.

I have taken my brother's words as a lesson in life. Sometimes when you get stuck, all you need to do is stay still and don't move. It seems we are all in a hurry to get out of bad situations we get ourselves into. You know the line of telling lies to get out of a lie…

In many of my conversations with people at 35,000 feet, I've counseled or advised them to stay where they are…evaluate the situation… see what got them there…don't be in such a rush…they could be heading into an even worse situation.

My brother made it out of Vietnam without one physical scratch on his body. He knew when to "stay stuck."

CHAPTER SIX

WE ALL KNOW SOMEONE

This conversation with the passenger in 2A really touched home for me, and I'm sure it will with many of you. The subject was about addictions. Many of my conversations at 35,000 feet have had something to do with a husband, wife, or a child that has become dependent on drugs or alcohol. This subject is ever-present in many of our daily lives, as we all have family members or friends that are affected by addictions.

The story is usually the same: he started out great, and then he got started with drugs and life changed; her schoolwork started declining; he lost his job and his focus. And usually the story involves some type of abuse.

After listening to a person's story, I normally begin to talk about my family's experience with my brother, who was on drugs, and a close friend, who still suffers from this addiction. When I say my close friend, I mean the family suffers. Addiction touches everyone, not just the individual with the addiction. My brother started at a young age, and he later went to jail for crimes associated with drug use. He could not break the addiction, and drugs finally cost him his life. He died at a young age.

I was about fifteen years old when my brother died, and can only remember the sadness it caused my family. I would sit and think that God had taken him to give my mother release from the years of problems he caused, as he was always in trouble and it always had something to do with his use of drugs. I also remember the love that my mother displayed until the end. I learned that a parent's love is unconditional and without limits. Even when my brother had put my mother through so much pain, she loved him. I think she felt that he needed her love more because he could not help himself.

This particular story is about an elderly lady in her early sixties. She and I began a casual conversation, and somehow the conversation turned to her son, who was a minister. I mentioned to her that I had thought at an early age that I too would take the path of becoming a minister, but after conversations with my mother, I decided not to take that course and at the young age of eighteen chose to join the military.

Our shared experience of serving in the military is the reason my brother was able to communicate about his service in Vietnam. He viewed me as a brother in arms, and he felt I understood where he was coming from. Actually, I could only relate a little to his challenges, as he served during a really tough time. I think I served my life calling well during my service to our country by mentoring and leading hundreds of young men and women. I still sometimes have the feeling that God is not finished with me in my call to the ministry.

The nice lady went on to share her son's story as she began to say that his life started out on a really bad path once he finished high school. He turned to drugs and was in and out of rehab facilities. He would be clean for a while, but he always went back to his drug addiction. He stole any- and everything he could get his hands on to pay for his drug addiction. Her husband finally said that he had had enough of trying to help him, as he was only using their love to keep up his lifestyle. Her husband kicked him out the house and told him to go lie to someone else.

The lady said this was the worst time of her life, as they would see him in the area on benches from time to time, and he was looking worse and worse. She and her husband would argue constantly about their decision, but in the end her husband would say their son could not come home until he wanted to get himself clean.

A few months passed, and apparently their son met a young lady who was also on drugs. But she lived in a house for drug addicts and brought this lady's son to this place to stay. It was run by a religious organization.

We talked about how much the religious community helps with social issues and we are very fortunate as a nation to have these organizations that, frankly, do for communities something the local or federal government can't do.

She said that one day, out of the blue, her son came by the house with his new girlfriend and he looked and acted different. She called her husband and told him of the visit. Her son told her that he was in a program and was doing better…she could see he was better. The staff members and volunteers at the facility were helping him and his girlfriend, and he had been drug-free for two months. They had helped him find a job, and he was working during the day to help pay for his room and board at the center.

The lady started to cry as she said that she remembered feeling so helpless with her son. The fact that he was now starting his way back and she had done what seemed like nothing to help him and was not a part of his recovery made her sad. I mentioned to her that she and her husband did what at the time was the only thing they could do. I said that, at that moment, her son's way to that center was through her and her husband's decision to let go. I told her that so often the answer is that simple—let go and let Jesus take the wheel. One of my favorite gospel songs is "Lay it down", by Troy Sneed. I have to remind myself of this simple act, as I can't solve every problem or situation that come across my path. So I told her she actually did help her son after all.

She told me, "Thank you for that point of view." We both by then had tears in our eyes.

She told me that each week her son would call, and they started to see that he was getting more serious with his girlfriend. They started to discuss marriage, but they realized they had a long way to go with their lives and addictions. Her son later started classes at the community college and went on to study theology. He and the young lady friend finally did get married, and now they have two children. She smiled and said, "My grandchildren." The lady told me that her son's life now is an absolute miracle, as she never imagined he would turn out to be half the man he has become. She thought that addiction to drugs had taken her son. She said, "He now gives most of his time to help those who, like him, have an addiction, because for anyone who has ever had an addiction, they know it is a struggle every day."

I told the lady that I believe in God know that all things are for a reason, even my brothers early death, which I attribute to his drug use.

The plane started its descent, and when we arrived at the gate, I give my new friend a hug and said good-bye.

I guess my mother's prayers for my brother were also for me. I witnessed the horrible tragedy of my brother's death and decided early that I would never allow drugs to be a part of my life. I instead pursued a life in law enforcement.

CHAPTER SEVEN

COLOR BLIND

The subject of religion is a taboo and often leads to disagreement during conversations. I also believe that racism and discrimination in America is also a difficult subject. But the subject always comes up during discussions.

With all the media attention and the controversy over immigration in America, race becomes a natural topic of discussion. And the fact that America has elected a black President, often gives passengers enough topics to debate for a fifteen-hour trip from Atlanta to Shanghai, China.

For the most part, I have been very impressed with the majority of people I have spoken to about racism and discrimination, regardless of their race. Most people seem to accept the fact that it is good for America and its principles to have finally elected a black President. But some people I've spoken with seem stuck on the fact that his name is Barack Hussein Obama. I recently had a conversation about President Obama's birthplace, and I told the person that I think it's embarrassing to most Americans that folks continue to make ridiculous assumptions about his birthplace. For God's sake, even when the man had been the president for almost four years, folks continued to question his birthplace.

Based on my conversations, I believe that, without a doubt, everyone loves our First Lady, Michele Obama. She represents Americans at their best. Her demeanor and open affection for Mr. Obama and their children is inspirational. Her project to inspire American children to be healthy through "Let's Move" is equally inspiring and worthwhile cause.

So, where do the folks in 2A stand on Mr. Obama? In my discussions, people seem to follow their party line, as Republicans say he is bankrupting America, and Democrats say any problems with the economy were caused by actions of past leaders.

As a black American, I am proud of President Obama's accomplishments. But I was against him before I was for him. I had been a Republican my entire adult life. During his campaign, a coworker and I were traveling together. When he came across a campaign pin for then-candidate Barack Obama, he tossed it to me. I said, "You can keep that one, as I'm a John McCain man," as I tossed it back to him. We laughed and he tossed it back to me. I placed it in my briefcase, thinking I would show it to my kids, as it was the first item I had held or seen of the candidate. Of course I still have that pin in my collection of President Barack Obama memorabilia.

I later started to listen to Barack Obama and found myself, along with millions of others, attracted to his message of hope and change. The thought that a black man could be president was still just a dream at that time. But as we all know, it became a reality.

Most passengers that I have conversed with really believe that they are not prejudiced against President Barack Obama because he is black, but because he is not doing a good job. I often fire back and say that I voted for President Bush twice, and thought he was good for America, until I started looking into the facts, and the facts don't lie. Was he the worst President ever? Did he not have any good moments and do any good for this country? Of course he did. So I often ask my friend in 2A, "Why can't we rate President Obama on the facts and the time he has had to do the work that needed to be done?" It seems as though many folks were only willing to give him a month, and if things were not better—if they did not see any change—they would say, "See there. He needs to go." Well, election 2012 has come and gone…and, yes, we will move forward. President Obama won four more years! Surly now the "birthers" and other folks will finally give him respect and support, right?

Oh, no, here we go again... He is going to take us off the "fiscal cliff."

Most black Americans, and minorities in general, including females, can identify with a self-imposed feeling of a double standard. All my life, I have thought that I needed to do things twice as well as my white counterparts. Please don't ask me why I felt this way, as no one ever told me I had to. Well, maybe my mother, Gladys, did. I've just always had a feeling that I have to be better; I must act better and be better to get the same evaluation as a white man. I'm sure my minority readers will agree to some extent. It is actually a common joke in the African American community. Let's say a white man commits a terrible crime and the story makes it on national television. Most in the black community would be heard saying, "He better be glad he wasn't black."

Another top issue that I discuss with my 2A passengers is immigration. Now, if you want to get someone in 2A going, just say that you feel for the Mexican immigrants and think that we need to address our national policies. You will get an earful, for sure. This, however, is exactly the way I feel on this issue. And I very well should, as my wife is a proud product of Mexico. And, no, she didn't come here illegally.

Many passengers in 2A will say that Mexicans are taking jobs from honest Americans and do not pay taxes. I often explain the real situation, which is that most Mexicans in America are working jobs that many honest Americans feel would not be good enough for them. Most Mexicans are honest and hardworking individuals simply trying to make money to feed, clothe, and shelter their families, which was impossible for them in Mexico. They choose the passage to America to pursue opportunity, as many of our forefathers did years past.

Many Americans seem to forget how America became a melting pot. In some cases, folks have the opinion that the pot doesn't need Mexicans boiling with the rest of us. I often point out another truth about the majority of the migrant workers and daily Mexican workers across America: For the most part, they buy their goods and services in

US cash, not credit. They pay taxes on goods and services, and many of course don't file income taxes. In the majority of cases, if they were here legally and filing income taxes, they would be due a refund from the government.

My last point on this issue is that many Mexicans residing in America are here legally. Many folks seem to want to label all Mexicans as illegal and ship them back to Mexico. I think we should embrace our Mexican friends and create better policies and procedures that ensure legal migration for work and citizenship. I feel it is equally important to create laws that protect their rights and safety in America. Many live and endure truly inhumane treatment because of the lack of government oversight and protection.

As I was writing this book, I wondered if I should include the discussion of race and immigration. But I decided it was important to create more discussion about the issue. I believe that we as Americans are still not where we need to be, but for sure we have come a long way. I do not want to minimize the problem of racial discrimination in America, though. If you ask many people from different ethnic backgrounds in America whether they have experienced racism or discrimination recently, a majority would likely say yes. Sometimes you can't explain it to the person that does not know, or has never dealt with it, but racism occurs everywhere in this country.

For example, an incident happened to me when I was staying at a very nice hotel in New York. Being a frequent traveler, I have been able to maintain diamond and platinum status at a few hotel properties. Therefore, using my status, I was staying in one of the best rooms available at traditional rates. That evening, as I was exiting my room to go have dinner, a white man in his sixties was exiting his room adjacent to mine. As we met in the hallway, without skipping a beat, he looked at me and said, "Could you bring some additional towels to my room?" I looked at him somewhat perplexed, as I couldn't understand what had given him the idea that I worked for the hotel. I then realized, "KJ, you are black."

So what could I say to the man who just assumed the only reason I was coming out of that room was because I must have just finished cleaning it. I did what many blacks and folks from different ethnic backgrounds do every day in America. I took the high road. I said to the man, "You know, if I hadn't paid the same or more for this room tonight, I probably would be the person to go get you some towels. But since I did, I can't help you." We ended up in the same elevator, and the man apologized for assuming I worked in the hotel.

When I tell this story to family and friends, I still can't believe it. My sister says I'm too nice and she would have told that man off. I tell her, "No, that's what people like him want us to do." Interestingly enough, a few of my white friends think it was no big deal. They say the nice man only made an innocent mistake and I should not have been offended... What do you think?

Some day I should play a joke on some white guy dressed as I was in a pair of dress pants, Allen Edmonds shoes, and a polo shirt. I would reverse the situation and ask him to bring me some towels. I wonder what his response would be. I am sure he would be equally perplexed... maybe more than I was, right?

When I decided to name this chapter "Color Blind," I mentioned to my daughter that I thought it would be cool if we all were color blind so we would not have an issue with racism. She immediately said, "If we were color blind, we would all see each other as black and white. Nothing would change. It's just putting everyone into a uniform."

I told her that that my definition of color blind is when we don't see any color and we treat people like my mother Gladys said we should: "Don't worry about what people look like. Instead, notice what they act like."

I can tell you that I was not acting like I worked at the hotel that evening. We have a long way to go, America. Let it start with you.

CHAPTER EIGHT

DR. KEN

As a senior enlisted officer in the military, I had many opportunities to counsel young enlisted members on everything from being deployed in a combat zone to needing money to buy groceries. You may or may not be aware of this, but America doesn't pay its military members that well. Many younger soldiers find themselves on food stamps and qualify for other economic assistance. I found that fact a little hard to believe myself, but it is true. We have come a long way since my early days, and the gap in pay compared to the civilian sector has gotten better. But it still has a long way to go.

I also counseled members and assisting personnel assigned to my unit on marital issues. They all wanted to know how to stay married. They thought this person was the greatest human on the planet just a few months ago, but now they couldn't stand to look at them. In the civilian workforce, most bosses do not counsel their staff on personal issues. But in the military it was a pretty usual activity. I thought that I was the Dr. Phil of my military unit; I guess I still do. The years of counseling seems to have prepared me for the variety of conversations with passengers that I have sat next to in 2A. Some were going through a rough spot in their marriage or trying to understand why all of a sudden when they forget to put the toilet seat down it was a felony offense.

Once, when I was on a trip to North Carolina, I called to check in with the family, and all my wife could talk about was that I had left the toilet seat up. In front of my business associates, all I could do was tell my wife how sorry I was and that I would never forget again.

Most of the conversations with men are discussions about how to manage traveling and home life. More and more, however, I'm seeing very successful businesswomen that are the breadwinners while their husbands are stay-at-home dads. Now, where was I when this became a common situation?

These businesswomen seem to be very proud and undeterred by being the breadwinner, and for the most part, they seem as though it's perfectly normal. I recall a time joking to one lady that if things didn't work out, I could make myself available. Yeah, I could be a stay-at-home dad, a well-kept man.

One passenger in 2A stands out as needing Dr. Ken. She was on her way from L.A. to Miami to see her fiancé. This sounds fair enough, but there was a big problem. She had only met this man on the Internet about five weeks earlier. He had introduced himself on a dating website as a fellow classmate. She said that she somewhat remembered him, but not really. A marathon of Internet and phone conversations led to their engagement and her being on the plane to meet up with him. If he turned out to be as she expected when she met him, she planned to return to L.A. to pack her things, relocate to Miami, and, yes, get married. She was a pretty lady in her mid-forties, and she seemed well-educated and had a good-paying job. She had been married before, but had been single for about five years.

I asked her two questions right away. First, of course, was, "Are you crazy?" My second question was, "Does anyone else know you are going to meet this guy?" She answered, "No, I'm not crazy, and yes, my parents know I am on my way down." I then asked her what his occupation was. Her answer made me laugh, but she didn't seem to catch the humor at first. She said that he was into pharmaceuticals sales. I tried to get this straight. I said, "So, he lives in Miami, and he sells drugs?" Again I asked her, "Are you crazy?" She then, got the point of my concern and admitted it all sounded a little out of the norm. We carried on a little more about her decision as the plane was landing. I thought for a moment and then handed her my business card. I told her that if she got into a situation and needed help to give me a call, as I was going to be in the area a few days. But I told her to call 911 first.

I never heard from her again, so I can only assume she is happily married to her drug dealer…I mean, pharmaceuticals salesman.

CHAPTER NINE

HE HAS A SECRET

This next story is somewhat strange. Remember, people talk to me all the time as if they have known me forever and can tell me their deep, lost secrets. Well, this story is another "relater experience."

My partner in 2A and I had started some small talk. I was talking about my wife and kids, and she told me that she had been married twice and had kids with her first husband, but her second husband and she had only been married for about two years. I told her that I too had been married twice, and that my first marriage didn't go as planned, but my second time around was a charm. She said her first husband had passed away after they had been married fifteen years. She had waited about five years and then decided to remarry. She said that she and her second husband got along great, and she loved him and he seemed to love her. But as time passed, a problem he had revealed itself. I thought, oh, here we go, he is a drug addict, or he cheated on her. So I sat back and waited. She looked at me and said, "Well, I never really tell anyone this, but he has a problem with sex."

I asked, "He can't have sex or is having difficulty?"

She said, "No, I wish that was the problem. We could have gotten that corrected with medication or whatever."

So I asked, "So what is his problem?"

She said, "Have you ever heard of people that like to self-gratify…?"

I wasn't sure I heard her correctly, so I asked, "What?"

She said, "Yes, self-gratify." She said that she hadn't known about this issue either. But she learned that others have this issue too—they prefer to sexually gratify themselves alone rather than have sex with their partner. She said for most young boys it happens as they are going through puberty, but they usually grow out of this activity. I, of course, was very surprised, as I had not heard of this phenomenon before, and I had never heard of it as the cause of a divorce.

So I said to her, "So his 'foreplay' was 'one play.'"

She laughed. She said it was hard to understand, but she did finally figure out what was really going on. She said she tried to discuss it with her husband. But it became a big problem, as she wanted a normal husband-and-wife relationship, which involved having a sexual connection. She said she finally couldn't take his behavior anymore and asked for a divorce. She said that at first she actually thought it was something wrong with her—that he just didn't want to have sex with her. But after time, she realized that he simply liked to self-gratify, and that was all he needed when it came to sex.

I was speechless. But I finally told her that, from what I could see, she was a very attractive woman and any man would be crazy to take self-gratification over her. Her marriage had ended over five years ago and she was in her late fifties. I asked her if she was planning to marry again. She said she hadn't ruled it out, but she was older now, and the experience really showed her that you don't know what you are getting into sometimes. She added that she enjoys being alone, and she has her two kids and one grandchild to keep her company. She said she did have a male friend and she was happy.

She then admitted that she was surprised she had told me her story. I told her that I was glad she had shared her story with me. I said it meant she had accepted the reality that there was not something wrong with her and it was best she had gotten out of the relationship.

I have found that all too often when someone's behavior goes against our mind-set, we try to think it's our fault, and then we think we can change the person. I have learned that in adult relationships, it is best to expect people to behave responsibly and reasonably. People make their own decisions and are accountable for their own actions.

This woman's husband should have told her up front about his sexual preferences. I also wondered while she was telling me the story why she didn't notice this behavior while they were dating. But we all know that, unfortunately, some things don't come out until after a few years of marriage.

I'm glad that she told "Mister Self-Gratifier" to hit the road.

CHAPTER TEN

WE ARE JUST PROCRASTINATORS

Am I the only one that hates to procrastinate? It seems that all the people I meet in 2A need to finish something—a project that they've been putting off and just can't finish. I asked my wife if she thought I would ever finish this book and get it published, and she replied, "You always finish what you start." I immediately pointed to a little crown molding job that I had started two years prior and had given up on with about a foot of space that needed to be completed.

For the record, crown molding is not as easy as it looks, and the area that has yet to be completed has about three corners. After wasting about twenty feet of expensive material, I finally admitted defeat. My plan was to hire someone to come and finish the job. But even in the worst of job markets, it would be hard to convince someone it's worth his time to come out to my house to do a one-foot crown-molding job. So there it sits, unfinished, until I decide to do another area of the house, which I plan to do someday. And then I will simply add that area to the job order.

So that's my procrastinating moment. We all seem to have something that we need to finish.

One passenger in 2A told me that she was headed to Florida, as she needed to finish going through her parents' things. Her father had passed away a year ago, and the house was just sitting. She had been trying to sell the house, and had finally got an offer. She told me that it was something that she had dreaded and couldn't wait until it was over. The memories of the life shared in the house with her parents were still very strong, and the thought of taking stuff out and disposing of it was very painful.

I told the 2A passenger that I sympathized with her and the tough task ahead. It is something that just has to be done, and the sooner she dealt with it the better.

As we get older, we start to realize the tough reality of life's fragility and the change of seasons. I really didn't get this point until my sister died in 2005 of cancer. She had requested that I say something at her funeral. So I got up to the podium and basically told everyone how proud I always was of my sister, as she had "made it." As a young woman, she was always very ambitious and strong. She left the small town we grew up in and headed for New York, where she became an administrator in a hospital. I remember saying to those gathered that as the youngest child of ten, growing up, I had never thought about my reality. But I now realized that as life ran its course, I would live to see many days like this: me at a podium talking about another sibling.

I guess that is why I generally do not put things off until tomorrow. I realize that tomorrow is not guaranteed for any of us, and we need to take the time to live, love, and do what is necessary today.

Now my wife has not quite adopted that philosophy, as she still has a project from fourteen years ago when our daughter was born. She started a knitting project for the baby; she was doing a quilt-kit project. It was supposed to be the ABCs. She started off motivated and full of energy. A, B, C, D…I remember seeing her knitting away and saying how our daughter was going to enjoy her beautiful blanket. Then she started skipping to the easy letters I, J, L, and finally to her last letter to date: T. I would tease her years later, saying that our daughter was going to grow up thinking the alphabet only has eight letters. When she was pregnant with our son, she got the bug again and started knitting another project: "Mi Casa, Su Casa."

Well, she managed to only finish the "Mi Casa," and finally gave up. She said, "They will know what should be next."

CHAPTER ELEVEN

WHAT'S YOUR OCCUPATION?

Now a surefire way to get the person sitting adjacent to me in 2A going is to ask the old favorite of air travel questions: "What's your occupation?" Sometimes it seems as though the person wants to say, "What took you so long to ask me? I am the president of such-and-such." I find that the men in 2A, to put it bluntly, love to brag. They can go on for hours about their jobs. They are so proud of their status, and most think they have a better position than I do. Sometimes when they finally ask me what I do, I want to say that I am the Under Secretary of State. I could easily pull it off with my world knowledge from my military background. Besides, no one knows who's the Under Secretary to anything, right? We know the current Secretary of State, as of November 2012, is Hilary Clinton. But, chances are, very few know who is the Under, Secretary of State.

By the way, one of them is William J. Burns, Under Secretary of State for Political Affairs. There are actually six Under Secretary of State Positions. There is one for Energy, Public Diplomacy, Management, and so on. And, no, I didn't know that until I looked it up to check the name. I thought, as most of you might, that there was only one.

Usually I just say that I am retired from the military and leave it at that so they can go on about themselves.

EXCUSE ME, I'M IN 2A

Over the years I have met people from every type of profession while traveling: senators, actors, actresses, NBA basketball players, physicists, boxers, wrestlers, doctors, lawyers, an owner of a septic tank company, businessmen and businesswomen, bull riders, bankers, and pharmaceutical reps...a lot of pharmaceutical reps. They seem to be everywhere.

Once on a flight headed to Los Angeles, I had a four-hour conversation with a lady in 2A who said she was in the entertainment industry. We talked about where we had lived, and I told her that I had lived in Hawaii. It turned out that she went to high school in the same small town where I had lived. We laughed and agreed it is a small world.

As we got more into her story, she finally told me that she was an actress and had been in a few major movies. I didn't recognize her, so I asked her to name one that I would know. She told me the name of one that happened to be playing on the flight entertainment system. I looked at the monitor, and there she was in the movie—big as daylight! I was so surprised and somewhat apologetic that I didn't recognize her. I had been just talking away to this big Hollywood star like we were old friends from yesterday.

When I told my wife who I had met and described our conversation, of course she didn't believe me. When I got home, she had searched for the actress on the Internet, and the bio she found backed up what I had learned through our conversation. The actress was not like I would expect a big star to be; she was really down to earth. Whenever I see her on TV, I tell my wife, "There goes my buddy." She laughs.

The conversation with the owner of the septic tank company was very interesting. I live in the country and actually have a septic tank... so let's just say I learned everything I needed to know and some things I would have been just fine without knowing about septic tanks. By the time our flight landed I was an expert at septic tank maintenance. When I got home, I took out the yellow pages and found someone to come out and give our system a check. I had learned on the flight that I should have it checked every three to five years. I must admit, prior to that flight, I had no idea how to maintain the system.

Maybe the next time someone asks me what my occupation is, I'll say I own a septic tank maintenance company. That will probably get the person to shut up and read the paper, right?

CHAPTER TWELVE

THE CRAZY THINGS PEOPLE DO AND WEAR ON A FLIGHT OR IN AN AIRPORT

As a frequent flier, I feel like I have seen it all on flights around the US and abroad. And if you are a frequent flier, you can attest to my thoughts on this subject.

Some things are just crazy, and others may fall in the funny and/or annoying category. Sometimes I want to say, "Did you know that you were coming to an airport or did you just happen to end up here by accident?"

An example of crazy might be the time I ran into a guy wearing pajamas. It would have been fine if he was a child between the ages of four and ten, and that's being generous. But this guy had to be around thirty years old. Everyone was staring. And he just headed down the corridor without a care in the world to, I presume, his departure gate. I thought maybe he was sleepwalking and would wake up Alaska, wondering how the heck he got there. A woman in her thirties galloping around the airport in her skimpy pajamas probably would have caused more of a stir, especially if she was attractive. I guess the guy made it through TSA screening without a problem.

According to an article dated July 19, 2011 in *USA Today's Road Warriors Survey*, frequent fliers have their gripes. Ten of them are:

1. people who carry on loud cell phone conversations;
2. people who disobey the rules and try to carry on too many bags or carry too much liquid through security;
3. people who play music so loudly that, even with earplugs or headphones, others can hear it;
4. passengers who show disrespect to flight attendants and gate personnel;
5. parents who don't try to control their children;
6. people who do not turn off electronics when they are asked to;
7. passengers who carry on and eat messy, smelly foods;
8. people who board with multiple or oversized bags and fill the bins in the front of the cabin when they're seated in the rear;
9. passengers who recline a seat in a tight coach cabin; and
10. people who leave a window shade open when the rest of the passengers have closed theirs and are trying to sleep.

The same article highlighted another interesting view. What annoys flight attendants? The Association of Professional Flight Attendants Union, which represents nearly 18,000 American Airlines flight attendants, listed ten annoyances:

1. walking around the aircraft without shoes, especially in the lavatory;
2. changing a diaper in the seat or on the tray table;
3. clipping fingernails and toenails on the aircraft;
4. keeping headphones on when talking to attendants;
5. speaking in a condescending and angry tone when it's not appropriate;
6. hanging arms or legs out in the aisle when the food and beverage cart is coming;
7. standing in the galley and restroom areas to stretch and do exercises;
8. keeping electronic devices on after the announcement has been made to turn them off;

THE CRAZY THINGS PEOPLE DO AND WEAR ON A FLIGHT OR IN AN AIRPORT

9. bringing stinky food on the plane; and
10. carrying on a bag too heavy to lift into the overhead bin.

You have probably seen most of these annoying actions of our fellow travelers. I don't think I would ever be guilty of clipping my toenails on a plane. What in the world were they thinking? How do attendants advise these people that it would be appreciated if they would discontinue their grooming activities? And regarding number ten on the list, I too get a little agitated when a little princess comes on with a hundred-pound bag and looks for her knight in shiny armor to save the day. The golden rule should be to never pack more than you can lift.

One flight attendant with over thirty-five years of service on a major airline told me that he would add one other annoying act of passengers. When he is serving beverages and a passenger says, "I would like a coffee." He then hands them the coffee and they say, "Can I have sugar?" He hands them the sugar, and then they ask for cream. He said after having that happen one hundred times a day, it gets a little annoying. He said, "Why can't they say, 'I would like a coffee with cream and sugar'?"

I must admit that I have had to be told to turn off my cell phone after the announcement was made a time or two. I will try to do better in the future…I promise.

CHAPTER THIRTEEN

THE CRYING CHILD

Now there probably is no more disturbing situation on an airplane then a child that is agitated and out of control. Having kids myself, I understand that those moments are going to happen. And sometimes, quite frankly, there is nothing to do about it but let them wail away until they stop and/or fall asleep. But on a plane this situation can be a real nightmare for everyone, especially the man in 2C—me.

I was on a flight that had what I would call a manageable situation. I call it "manageable" because, in my opinion, the parents could have handled the problem of their crying child better.

A man and a woman had boarded with their daughter, who was four or five. As they found their seats, they decided that the child would sit with the husband a few seats back, and mom would sit alongside me in 2A. Throughout the boarding process, the kid was giving her dad a really hard time and was crying very loud and at some points yelling, saying that she wanted her mom. You could hear the dad saying, "No, honey, you are going to sit with me. Mom is right there, and it's OK." The little girl was really letting it out, and the mom next to me had taken out a bag with what looked like a Philly cheesesteak sandwich. I was thinking, "You need to put that sandwich down and go get that child." She looked at me and said, "We are trying to teach her that she can't be with me all the time and must stay with her dad when we tell her to." I told her I understood and that children are little demons at times. She agreed and continued with her sandwich.

The flight finally departed, and, seriously, that little girl had been crying throughout the entire boarding process. At this point, everyone was looking around as if they couldn't believe the flight attendant had not intervened. I'm sure we were all hoping this would not be allowed to go on for the entire two-hour flight.

The lady then said that she was sorry and she should go console her daughter. I said to myself, "No, you need to go back there and spank some butt."

I could only imagine me putting on such a show with my mother, Gladys. Man, she would have probably killed me right there on the plane with all those witnesses. And she would have said her famous words: "I brought you in this world, so I can take you out." She said that often. We all believed her too.

Gladys more than likely, however, would have pulled out her "whipping strap." This was one thing that dad did for us in the way of discipline. He made sure Ms. Gladys had her supply of straps. He got them from his work. A conveyor belt in the factory where he worked often broke, and the leather straps had to be replaced. He would bring the old broken straps home. They would be cut down to about ten inches long and maybe two inches wide. Ms. Gladys really used these straps to maintain order in her house.

We didn't have 911 emergency services, or the discipline of a simple "time out" to save us, so we were at the mercy of Ms. Gladys, who handled us kids misbehaving in her own way: "the strap." She would make us go get it, too. She had a weird payback system, as well. She would say "I'm going to pay you for old and new." So we often didn't know if we were getting spanked for something we just did, or if we had done something a few days ago that she suddenly decided to discipline us for.

Once when I was twelve or thirteen years old, I had done something wrong. It was some small infraction I'm sure, as I was a very good kid and seldom got spankings. She told me, "Go get my strap," so she could give me the usual two or three swings of her strap.

She would make us hold out either hand, and then she would give us a big slap on the hand with the strap. She expected us to keep our hand out and not pull back, even though we knew we were about to get what felt like a bolt of electricity. On this occasion, I got a little jittery and pulled my hand back, and the strap hit my mom's leg. She said, "Look at what you made me do." I wanted to say, "No, look at what you just did. If you would stop swinging this strap like a mad woman this would not have happened." But of course I only said, "I am sorry." And she gave me an extra swing of the strap for making her hit herself.

So my 2A partner was back behind me, telling her daughter to listen and be quiet. She told the little girl to remain with her dad. I thought the woman was going to start counting to ten at any moment.

The little girl was crying and saying, "No, no, I want to come with you."

The other passengers were obviously now very frustrated. Many looked at the flight attendant to do something. After the woman came back to 2A, the flight attendant approached her and said, "Miss, I think everyone would appreciate it if you would go sit with your daughter so she can settle down." The lady said that they did not want to give into their daughter's demands because they did not want to handle their daughter's acting out by "letting her have her way." The flight attendant said what I'm sure we all had wanted to say for about forty minutes: "This is not the place to be trying to train your daughter to behave. Please do everyone a favor and go sit with your daughter."

The lady finally agreed, and the husband came up and sat by me in utter defeat. I told him that I had kids and know they can be trying, but everyone on the plane was about to drag his wife back to his daughter. He laughed and told me that he actually had told his wife to sit with their daughter, knowing how she was so attached to her mother. But his wife had insisted that he sit with his daughter. The wife did seem to have a type A personality, and the husband was a little on the mild side. I told him about my mother, Ms. Gladys, and he laughed again. When the plane landed, I asked him if he was going to go out and get himself a "strap." But for some reason I don't think so…

As for me, I have learned to take a middle ground between the strap and reasoning with our children. You know the old adage, "spare the rod and spoil the child." Well, I do believe that it takes strong discipline to get young children's attention. It's important to establish ground rules along with use of "time outs." I often tell my children about their grandmother, and they surely don't want to get to that level. So our children know not to push our buttons too hard.

I must admit that my own style of discipline didn't come without some retraining through books from parenting skills experts, such as Donna G. Corwin. My kids owe a lot to this lady, as she would never promote the use of "the strap."

CHAPTER FOURTEEN

HONEY, PUT THE SEAT DOWN

This is not a hot topic for men that are newly married, as putting the toilet seat up or down usually doesn't come up until after the honeymoon phase. Newly married people are still so madly in love with each other that they don't want to start putting down rules and making demands.

I think my wife waited until we had been married for about two years before she started telling me all the things she didn't like so much about me. Her number one complaint was that I didn't put the toilet seat down after using the restroom. It seems that most of my men friends in 2A also did not get the proper house training in this area of home life, which gives us many laughs. We often wonder why our moms didn't teach us about this, but maybe they were so proud that we learned to lift the toilet seat up that they didn't want to ruin a great accomplishment with more demands. At first I thought my wife was joking when she brought up this "big problem." I thought, "What could she want me to put the seat down for? For crying out loud, I did lift the seat like any thoughtful guy should. Besides, for the last twenty-eight years I had followed Gladys's rules of lifting the seat before using the restroom, and she had been happy with that. What was my wife now requiring of me? Was she trying to express some type of control over me? Or was it the beginning of her trying to domesticate me?

Well, through my travels in 2C, I soon found that I was not the only man to have this big problem at home; so did all the men in America and probably the world. Once my wife called me and was giving me the fifth degree about the toilet seat not being down. I responded, "Honey, I'm sorry. But what can I do now? I'm in South Carolina working to help pay the mortgage. If you could be so nice just this time and let it down, I promise I won't do it again." Do any of you guys relate to this craziness?

The years have now gone by with many arguments over this issue, and now I feel like I could have a master's degree in this area. But a few years back something happened that would bring a smile to many men's faces.

My wife calls me into the bathroom, and without a twitch, she said, "You didn't close the lid."

I said, "What are you talking about?"

She said, "You will never get it, will you?"

I said, "Honey, I know I let the seat down. I have it right here on my iPhone: 'Note to Kenny—let seat down."

She went on, "You are just awful… You did put the seat down, but you left the lid up."

I said, "The lid…I thought the deal was to put the seat back down. So now the new rule is the lid must be down too…"

So if you are a newlywed, take my advice and get a jump on this. Start letting the lid down…it will save you a lot of headaches. By the way, I have taught my son to do the same. He will probably never realize the great gift I gave him by doing this.

Most of the guys in 2A agree with me that the issue is a little petty. But one day I got a taste of my own medicine. We were finishing dinner, and I had had a few drinks and was feeling pretty good. Later I had to take care of my business, so I went in the restroom and without looking just sat right down. You girls know what happened. That's right, the seat was not down. Since I'm not the widest-bottom guy in the world,

I thought for sure that I would fall right in. I give out a big laugh, and when I went back out to my wife, I said, "I almost fell in the damn toilet. Don't forget to let the seat down. No, better yet, make sure you put the lid down while you're at it." She laughed, and I think that was the end of the old toilet seat problem for us.

CHAPTER FIFTEEN

EXPECTATIONS

Many people who reviewed this book or heard my ideas told me to name it "Friends." Obviously, I kept my original idea, *Excuse me, I'm in 2A*, which I think is a pretty good title. The idea of calling it "Friends" is equally fitting, though, and therefore deserving of some attention.

The many people I wrote about in this book are probably not my friends in the strict sense of the word. But if I saw them again, I'm sure we would say hello and be friendly and talk about how we've been and so on and so forth... like we have known each other forever. But I imagine a few of my 2A friends would not remember me at all, even though they divulged some deep secrets, as they were just passing the time on our two-hour flight.

A few of my 2A seatmates told me that they were traveling to visit with a friend and some were returning from a visit. One person told me he was very glad to be on the plane going home because he had spent the last three days visiting with a long-ago friend who only wanted to talk about the things they did when they were in college. My seatmate said it was as if his friend had been in a time capsule and nothing had changed; he was living in the past. He said that he was disappointed because they had communicated on the phone and Internet leading up to his visit, and he had been excited about the visit. His expectations were high.

I'm sure you have friends like that. You pay a visit back home for whatever reason and you run into some old buddies. You might even go out to dinner. And all they want to talk about is stuff that happened twenty years ago. When you try to interrupt one of their stories from long ago to interject some more recent events, such as the fact that Mr. Obama won the presidential election, they look at you as if you are an alien trying to ruin the moment.

Years ago when I would return home from my assignment with the army, I would meet up with the old gang. I actually found myself watching what I said or brought up, as I didn't want to sound like a show-off with my newfound knowledge of something that didn't originate in Heath Springs, South Carolina.

Later I found out from one of my old friends that he actually wanted to hear of my adventures. He asked me why I didn't talk about my travels, as he found it very interesting and exciting to hear, especially since he had never had the opportunity.

I still have true friends that live in my old town and have never left. But through the years, I still choose not to talk about my career and travels away from my small town. I prefer to talk about the family and catch up on local happenings, which for me is very interesting and I really enjoy catching up on all the local news.

My other friends that I have met along life's pathway have not always been long-lasting. However there are a few that I am still close to. For example, I have a deep brotherly friendship with someone I served in Germany with, and I must say that I love that guy. I also have a buddy from my days as a drill instructor in Alabama. We call each other twice a week and have been friends for over twenty years.

Like most people, however, some of my friendships didn't always work out so well and I found myself "cutting them loose." That's the term I use when someone turns out not to be the kind of friend I thought he was. I'm sure our expectations of each other got in the way. Let's face it, sometimes we find friends in weird ways, and we quickly realize they are not our buds after all. We feel like we need to put a little space between ourselves and our new friends.

EXPECTATIONS

There's that line about friends in the bar: "after midnight, everyone in the bar is your friend." Perhaps that is true, especially after a few shots of tequila. But I wouldn't call one of those bar friends the next day and expect him to drop everything and come help me with a flat tire. He probably wouldn't even remember who I was...

I might call someone my friend after he has done something for me or helped me, especially if it's happened more than once. But, trust me, this is not the best way to identify someone as a friend, as many people will do one nice act but then expect a lifetime of good deeds in return.

When I was living in Germany or on other foreign assignments, locals explained to me that they didn't understand the American manner of acting so "friendly." They asked me why Americans always wave and say hello to everyone we meet. And these folks from other countries said it was especially funny when we ask someone we don't know, "How are you doing?" They wondered: If everyone was so nice and friendly in America, why did the news show Americans being murdered every day? I must admit that I totally understand this opinion, and I think we Americans are somewhat fake in our concerns for each other.

For me, growing up in the South, I'm especially guilty of superficial friendliness. Where I grew up, it was just common practice to say hello and ask everyone, "How are you doing?" We usually didn't wait for a response, because we knew the usual answer would be, "Fine. And you?" Then later in the evening, we sat on the porch and discussed the real deal on everyone. Who was sick, who was going to jail, who just passed away... Sometimes I would be surprised at this one, because I just saw that person a day or two ago and she told me she was "fine."

I've used the word *expect* a lot when referring to friends, as I guess that what friends often do—we expect things from each other. Sometimes when we do something or attempt to help people, we expect them to appreciate our actions. . Well, this is not always the case, as in the following situation.

A few years ago I was waiting in line at the ticket counter at the airport, as usual. A lady in line ahead of me, about forty years old, was asking the ticket agent to exchange her ticket, as she had missed her flight. The ticket agent told the woman that she couldn't exchange the ticket at the counter and she needed to call the customer service helpline for assistance.

The lady told her story another time and again asked the ticket agent to give her another ticket. Again, the ticket agent told her that she needed to call customer service line instead. The lady started to tell the agent her story for the third time. At this point I decided to see if I could help the agent. So I tapped the lady on her arm and told her that, from what I had heard three times from the agent, she needed go call the customer service center for assistance with her problem.

Well, even though I thought I was assisting the agent, she said to me, "Sir, you need to mind your own business. I am helping this lady. Please wait your turn." I looked at the agent in surprise. And then the lady took her turn at me and said, "Yeah, you need to mind your own business." I thought "Kenny, that's what you get for trying to be helpful." So I waited, and finally the lady got the message and went over to the phone. And I was able to get my ticket from the agent without saying a word. My expectations in this situation of course were not met, as I thought I was being helpful and the ticket agent would be grateful for my assertion.

We all experience similar situations in our friendships and with our acquaintances. And sometimes when people fail to live up to our expectations, our relationships can be damaged. Sometimes the people we meet are just being nice and are not looking to be our friends. Our expectations of people will not always be met. I have found that the best way to go about my daily life is to be myself and accept the fact that my actions are done with my own purpose and others do not know the reasons for my actions. The people I interact with are not necessarily going to match my behavior or live up to expectations.

I admit this is not easy to do. We all have expectations of others, right? I remember once my wife and I were sitting in a small local bar watching a ballgame. A guy sat to my left, and I stood beside my wife, who was seated.

Another guy sat to my left, about two seats over, with a lady who was also standing.

EXPECTATIONS

Later, the guy to my immediate left got up, so I then had a seat. But instead of sitting down, I offered the chair to the man with the lady that was standing. He didn't respond to me. My wife asked me what I had said to the guy, and I told her that I had offered him the seat. My wife told me to sit down and stop being so polite. So I sat down next to her.

Moments later, my wife had to use the restroom. As my wife left, the man that I had offered the chair to came over and moved my wife's chair away from me. I of course looked at the man and asked him why he was moving my wife's chair. He said, "Because you need to move down." I said, "Who are you to be making someone move down?" He walked away and came back with a man who identified himself as security and told me I had to leave the bar.

Now that's what I got for being Mr. Nice Guy. It turns out the guy who took my wife's chair was the owner of the bar. And my wife, who had arrived back to her seat to learn we were being asked to leave the bar, had observed the owner's lady friend looking in our direction. My wife had observed them having what seemed like heated discussion before she went to the restroom. I told my wife that maybe the lady was eying her and now this idiot had gotten jealous and his response was to get rid of his competition.

No, we never went back to that bar.

So my advice to my 2A partner is not to expect people to act or react the way you might expect, because you never know…

But I must admit, when someone's actions do live up to my expectations, I feel a sigh of relief that someone finally has some common sense…

CHAPTER SIXTEEN

WHERE ARE YOU FROM?

The one question often asked when people first meet and this is especially true on an airplane: "Where are you from?"

When I decided to join the military, which of course , boy, that was a life-changing decision. I will talk more about that in a later chapter. For the purpose of this chapter, however, I mention my service because until that time I had not been to many places besides my hometown. For the most part, I only knew two types of people—black and white—and most of the people I knew were family. We all looked alike, and we surely talked alike. Now I've been away from Heath Springs, South Carolina where I grew up for over thirty years.

I'm not sure whether it's true or not, but they say my town got its name from the healing springs that once were naturally there. People would come from all over to bathe in the springs. The baths were said to relieve whatever pain their bodies were experiencing. In 2011 the town's population was 794. The town has only a "caution light" and a few stores. When my kids ask me if they can do something crazy, I'll say, "Where am I from?" and they know that means the answer to their question is *no*.

When I take my children to my hometown and they visit with the locals, my kids often ask me, "Daddy, what did they say?" I have to do my best job of translating, as I have lost most of the country dialect and consider my speech somewhat clear. But my kids would disagree and say that when return to my home town, I revert to my roots.

When I was younger, I was always amazed that people could always guess where I was from. I would often ask them, "How do you know?" They would probably look at me like I was crazy, but I was too young and naïve to about dialects. On the other hand, I could never guess where people were from, as I had never heard most of the accents. I could usually guess New Yorkers, but that was about it.

Now that I have traveled to almost every state and most countries, I am very good at guessing where people are from before they tell me. I wait until they verify my assumption as to where they are from, and usually I'm right.

One day a nice older gentleman sat beside me in 2A, and we exchanged hellos. As we spoke, I could pick up his obvious German accent. He told me he was from Frankfurt, Germany, and I informed him that I had spent six years in Germany and actually had good conversational knowledge of the German language. He looked very surprised, but I started speaking German, and we continued the conversation in his native language.

My German was a little rusty, but it was enough to still amaze the gentleman. He then asked me where I was from, and I told him South Carolina. To my surprise, he was now living and working in South Carolina. He told me that he really loved the South, but he thought it was still a little behind the times in terms of equality. He realized soon after he arrived that there was still tension between blacks and whites there.

I told him about an experience I had when I returned from an overseas assignment in South Korea and was at the time stationed at Ft. Jackson in South Carolina. This was around 1984. I had gone to buy a piece of furniture from a local store and had come to a decision on an item. The salesman and I had actually completed the transaction, which was a cash deal, and I reached out my hand to, as they say, "seal the deal" with a handshake. The man looked at me with a confused look and refused to shake my hand. I will never forget the feeling that situation gave me as a man. I looked at the salesman and said, "You know, I just changed my mind. Please cancel the sale and give me back my money." The man looked even more confused and asked me, "What's the problem?" I just said, "Nothing. I just changed my mind." The German man seemed to understand the affect that situation had on me still. He said, "I can only imagine how that made you feel."

I went on to tell him how my wife and I loved Germany. We had many wonderful experiences there, and our daughter was actually born in Germany. And my older son from my previous marriage was born there as well. My partner in 2A laughed and said, "I think you and I have much in common, as I also have two children that were born in Germany." We laughed and talked more about the good beer and wine in Germany and of course the festivals that seem to never end.

So we two men, from two different countries, at first assumed we had nothing in common. By the end of a two-hour flight, however, we realized that we shared a kinship for each other's homeland—him for South Carolina and me for Germany.

CHAPTER SEVENTEEN

I LOVE MUSIC

If I could have been anything in my life, I know I would have been a musician—maybe a singer or a guitarist. Some say I have a pretty good voice. You can find me on any given Saturday night at a local bar in my town singing karaoke. I think music is a perfect way to calm down after a hard day. And the musicians who make us reflect or make us just want to dance are truly god sent.

Many of my 2A friends have been surprised to find out as we discussed music that I really enjoy country music…good country music… in the style of Willie Nelson, Julie Roberts, Brooks and Dunn, and guys like Jason Aldan, Darius Rucker, and Kenny Chesney. I think I like him because his name is Kenny…

Once a white lady in her early fifties was seated in 2A listening to her music. I could hear a little, as the volume was somewhat loud. She dressed as though she was a businessperson. To my surprise, she was playing what sounded like Lil Wayne—a popular rapper. Later into our flight, I said to her, "So, you are into rap music." And she said, "Oh, yes. I like the way they tell their stories. I like the stories of their struggles and their love of life." She said, "They are just so real."

She described how inspiring to hear the way many rapper's rap about their humble beginnings and their life lessons. I thought this lady was very cool, and I was impressed that she really displayed a true love of rap music and what many rap artists try to do in their songs. I admitted to her that I was surprised by her choice of music, and she said, "Why?" Again she got me with that response. I went on to say I guess my assumption of her when I first saw her would be that she would prefer classical music. She said, "Hell no." I told her that I too am a fan of rap music, but not the hard-core stuff. I said I often found it necessary to get the "clean" version, as I had little ones at the house. I told her that my favorites were Mary J. Blige, Missy Elliott, Eminem, and Jay Z. My 2A partner then told me that in her opinion, "Eminem is a genius."

I told her that my favorite music, however, was country music. I enjoyed their stories and the honesty found in the music. I shared with her a few more of my favorites such as Reba, Sugarland, Tobe Keith. The lady admitted that she didn't know much about country music and didn't enjoy that style of music.

I guess the story that is being told here is that we often make judgments about people based on their ethnicity, where they are from, or their age. On this flight, most people would have assumed my 2A friend and my tastes in music would have been reversed.

The truth is music has no boundaries. Different genres of music can be enjoyed by anyone from any ethnicity, financial background, and religion. I find that music and the musicians that make it are truly "color blind."

CHAPTER EIGHTEEN

I AM PROUD TO HAVE SERVED

The conversation topic that fills me with the most pride is the twenty years that I served in the United States Army. When I share with my 2A friend that I served in the military, they always say, "Thank you for your service." I usually will say, "I am proud to have served."

My career in the military is one that almost wasn't. But Gladys told me to stick with it, as I had made the commitment to serve. I joined the military to be a military policeman in 1980. The army recruiter did a fine job, showing me the pretty uniforms the military policemen wore and guys performing White Hat or Garrison police duties. He forgot to show me the majority of the duties of military police units, which was combat or field service. My first assignment and many to follow was the later, combat MP units.

My first assignment after military police training at Fort McClellan, Alabama, was with the 7th Infantry Division at Fort Ord, California. I arrived there in 1981 a naïve eighteen-year-old boy from Heath Springs, South Carolina. I thought all my sergeants were on drugs and alcohol, which many were. And they swore and spoke the Lord's name in vain with every sentence that came out of their mouth. I called my mother and told her that I had made a big mistake All we did was go to the field and were nothing more than combat troops, and we never did the police work that I thought I had signed up for. Ms. Gladys would hear none of my complaining and crying. She told me that I needed to hang in there and honor my contract. She reminded me that it was my idea to join and she never wanted me to enlist. I told her that the devil was everywhere here and I didn't fit in. She told me that if that was the case, I had many souls to save and needed to get to work spreading the word of Jesus to all those sinful men.

Well, I stopped complaining and started to try and find the good side of my situation. That wasn't all that hard to do, as we were in California near beautiful Monterey, California. My new friends and I would go to the beautiful Fisherman's Wharf and Carmel-by-the-Sea. I found that I really loved the ocean. Even thought I grew up in South Carolina, which has plenty of coastlines, I really didn't spend much time near the ocean. As a kid in South Carolina, I think I had been to the beach only once.

I later had the opportunity to join the unit's special reaction team. I really enjoyed being a part of this very elite group of physically fit and excellent marksmen. We received specialized training, and I soon began to feel more accepted, as I was very athletic and a very good shot with all the weapons. I started to get recognized for my good attitude and willingness to go out of my way to help everyone. And guys in general thought I was "squared away," which is military jargon meaning I was a good MP. In no time at all, I was promoted to E3, Private First Class. I found that I enjoyed the service and the combat MP unit. About every three months, we did do routine police duties similar to what local policemen would do, as a military installation is like having a small city within a city. We had to go break up a lot of bar fights, and there were plenty of domestic disturbances. The infantry soldiers would go away for weeks on end. And when they returned, they often found that their loved ones were not waiting faithfully for them at home, and we would have to go into their homes and calm the situation. Life was tough for these men between the ages of nineteen to twenty-five (the infantry only have men assigned). They often had little to no family support to help with the problems of being young and married.

Their young wives really had it tough. At least the husbands had the members of their unit as friends, but the wives were often new to the area with no one to assist them with day-to-day problems. The military units had what's known as family support groups, but the young ladies would not always find it comfortable to go to strangers for assistance. This situation caused the military to have a high divorce rate.

As a young MP, I took note of this situation in the military. And I used my awareness of the problem later as a leader. My wife and I were very active with our younger members and their spouses. We tried to ensure that they knew we were aware of their situations and would provide whatever assistance they needed, which was often only someone to listen.

My years of service went by it seems now too quickly. I often say I can't believe I served for twenty years and had the opportunity to make a difference in so many individual lives.

I later went on to earn my college degree and got promoted. I often tell people that I probably got promoted five times too many, as I was a darn good Private First Class (E-3). The army and my leaders above me, however, saw something in me. And when it came time to retire, I had earned the rank of E-8, First Sergeant.

I traveled and served in many locations, both overseas and here in the United States, including Bosnia, Germany, Hawaii, Japan, Korea, Alabama, California, Florida, and South Carolina. I would typically stay at a location for two to three years. When I ask my wife these days if she would like to move, she says, "No. We've done enough of that for a lifetime."

I'm often asked about my best and worst assignment. I usually say that as I look back, they all were a special place and time in my life. My time as a drill sergeant in Alabama, however, was a highlight of my time in service. I had the ability and opportunity to help many young men and women get their lives started in a new direction. I enjoy telling stories from my time as a drill sergeant. One story that always comes to mind is the time the company commander had to come out and ask my group, we called it a platoon, which consist of approximately fifty personnel to stop their chant. When training starts the drill sergeant get all the members of the platoon together and together they decide on a chant that they say together for motivation. My platoon this time came up with the phrase, "We get paid to do the wild thing." Every time I or another drill sergeant that worked with me would call the platoon to attention, which basically means everyone stops moving and talking and looks straight forward and listens for further instructions. We had been together for probably a week by the time the commander heard our new chant, and on this occasion the commander was in the area. I called the platoon to attention, and there they were, all fifty of my young women, yelling at the top of their lungs, "We get paid to do the wild thing". The commander came running over, drill sergeant, drill sergeant. We can't have these girls going around the installation yelling, "We get paid to do the wild thing." We need to change that now. It was the funniest thing ever, as until he said it the way he did, I never thought the chant might be a little inappropriate for a group of young ladies. Hey, to me they were my young soldiers. The commander and I would always recall that situation for months to come and would always laugh hysterically at the situation, whenever we met. To make matters worse, when the platoon finished training and were preparing to graduate, they called me in to their living area and presented me with a plaque, which said, "Thanks Drill Sergeant Cauthen for your motivation and commitment. We get paid to do the wild thing - 3rd Platoon Bulldogs." We had changed the chant to "Always Forward."

My time as a first sergeant, which I served on two separate occasions, was also a definite highlight of my army career.

Often my 2A seatmate, as well as friends that know me in general, will ask me about my combat time. And I tell them that I was very fortunate, and, out of my twenty years in the military, I only served for about a year in a combat zone. During that time my wife and I wrote letters to each other every day, which she still has locked up in a safe place. Many people ask me about my view of war. My response is that war is not the ultimate answer, but unfortunately it is sometimes necessary.

I would like to say on behalf of all of my fellow veterans: "We are proud to have served."

CHAPTER NINETEEN

THERE IS A TIME AND A SEASON FOR EVERYTHING

In an earlier chapter I alluded to my Christian faith and mentioned that I would discuss it in another session. So there's no time like the present.

At times, I have found myself engaged in this very personal conversation with my 2A friends. Many, I find, are as I am and have a deep and personal religious faith.

I gained my faith in Christ as a young child. My mother would make sure we went to church every Sunday. It was not ever up for discussion. We knew that no matter what we did the day before, come Sunday morning we were at Sunday school, and then on to regular church services. I grew up attending Methodist services and received Christ as my Lord and Savior through the Methodist church rituals.

I also sang on the church choir. Now, I consider myself a pretty good singer. But at the time I was very shy and just stood in the background and sang along with the other young men. We had our superstar singers, and we sure had a great time singing and praising the Lord.

My kids still enjoy my stories about the older ladies in my church who would get "in the spirit." The first time I saw it, I thought someone should be helping the lady, as she must have been having some type of attack. If there had been 911 services back then, I probably would have dialed it for help.

The person on her feet would be experiencing a physical and very real connection with the spirit, and the other ladies would encourage her and tell her to, "Go ahead, let it out." Actually the entire church would join in when someone was "receiving the spirit." The choir would really get going, and everyone would have a real old-fashioned religious experience. I look back on those days, and the memory still moves me.

My wife grew up Catholic, so we agreed to raise our kids as Catholics. Catholic Church services are very different from my childhood experience of church, to say it mildly. But I think it is important for us to attend church together.

I was on a flight a few years ago, and the topic of religion came up somehow out of nowhere. The passenger beside me stated that he was an atheist, and he didn't believe in God.

I was quiet for a minute. As I recall, the weather was causing turbulence, and the plane was bouncing around probably more than I had ever seen. A lady across the aisle was holding a cup of coffee, and all of a sudden one of the bigger bumps of turbulence hit. I watched her coffee go up in the air, and the coolest thing happened—I could actually see the full cup of liquid as it suspended in air for a split second before it came splashing down all over her. Her husband next to her had just given me a friendly smile, but his face fell as he realized his wife was covered in coffee.

I wondered why, of all days, I had to get stuck with an atheist beside me in 2A this day. I said a quick prayer, advising God that I wasn't ready to go yet, and that we needed to give this atheist a little more time to come to Christ. I guess God was listening, as we made it to our destination safely.

The old saying in the military is, "There are no atheists on the battlefield." I think the same should be true for being on an airplane at 35,000 feet.

I have never tried to convert anyone to my views about religion. But I have been known to offer my experience and advice, which most of the time have a Christian view. I certainly can't judge others, because over the years I have said and done things that I'm not too proud of and were none-to-Christian.

I decided to include a chapter about my faith, as I really believe and have come to realize that, "to everything there is a season and a time." The Bible talks about this in Ecclesiastes 3:1.

I do have a worldly opinion about things based on my experiences, but I have come to see life in the text of Ecclesiastes 3:1. We all know that generally a baby is going to be born when it's good and ready, no matter what the doctor has told the anxiously waiting parents. One night, the mother-to-be will get up and say those famous words, "The baby is coming!" The father will, of course, say, "What? Are you sure? It's not time yet." We men don't realize how dumb we must sound when we say such things… When it's time, it's time. And at this moment, the wife knows she is about to have that baby…period. No matter what the doctors said seven and half months ago.

The opposite end of this amazing life cycle is, of course, death. In my experience, it is equally as untimely and unexpected.

I told you about my brother, who served in Vietnam. He was serving over there in absolute chaos, and he made it home without a scratch. It wasn't his time. He later died of cancer at the young age of sixty-one. It seems unfair; you would think that my brother, who made it through what must have seemed like hell and sacrificed so much, should have been rewarded with a long, healthy life. But it doesn't work that way.

I wrote in chapter six about drug additions: "We All Know Someone." I mentioned my brother and how drugs changed his life and because of the path he choose it lead to him making decisions that caused him his life. The use and abuse of drugs have taken too many of our brothers and sisters.

So let's not waste the seasons and the time we have, as many of us do. Live your life with humility and respect for others. Let's all pledge to be "color blind." If there is someone out there suffering with an addition to drugs or alcohol, make the tough decision to seek help. Realize that you more than likely can't fight the addition on your own.

Parents, guardians be good role models for your children and find honor in your sacrifice for them, it's your responsibility. I'm always respectful when I see a young, single mother, who is perhaps going to school and working while raising a child with little to no help. The same can be and is true for a few fathers that have also found themselves in this position.

Children, you are the future. Respect your talents. Don't be deterred by your inabilities, but have the mind-set to concentrate and capitalize on your abilities. By doing so, you will find that you can always overcome your inabilities.

I felt my time to write this book had come. As the years have passed, and as I have been gathering information and actually writing this book, many everyday events have taken place that have touched on points I wanted to highlight in this book. Relevant matters don't change overnight. And if someone writes about something important today and someone reads the words ten years from now, surely a headline in that day's paper would be about the same issue.

I ask you to join me in saying that it is time for the season of racism in America to come to an end. I've alluded to many incidents of racist or prejudiced behavior that I have experienced over the years. And, believe me, there have been many more. For example, a white man told my wife—who is Mexican and was walking in the Wal-Mart parking lot with our daughter and speaking to her in Spanish—to go back to her country. My daughter of course asked her mother, "What country is he talking about? We are in our country, right?" My wife told our daughter that the man was ignorant and not to worry. My wife told my daughter that they can speak Spanish anytime and anywhere they want.

We as nation need to stand together and say enough is enough. There is a rule about passing by a mistake and not correcting it. It's said that by doing so you accept that mistake as being proper or correct. In other words, your non-action makes a statement that something inacceptable is acceptable. Each time you allow yourself or someone in your presence to speak or act in a racist manner, you have accepted that behavior as proper and are equally responsible. I don't speak of anyone and refuse to allow anyone around me to speak in a prejudicial or unkindly manner about persons of another race.

I challenge you to do the same. We can make a difference. The time is now for the season of racism to come to an end.

ACKNOWLEDGMENTS

Where does one start with the acknowledgment of those who have been such an inspiration for this book? I must start with my mother, Gladys. As you have seen, she is still very much a part of me. I think I have always paid respect to her and her influence on my life, but until now I have never seen it spelled out the way it comes through in the book. Gladys passed away in 2001, but her lessons and simple manner in which she lived her life lives on; hopefully you will gain from her perspective.

I would be remiss if I didn't acknowledge my wife of eighteen years. She took on the responsibilities and role not many would have accepted, that of a military spouse. She never doubted my abilities, and she gave me the strength to hold my head up through the years. What they say is true: beside every great man is a greater woman. I thank you for your steady and constant trust and confidence throughout the years—as Gladys would say, "through thick and thin."

Finally, I thank the folks that are in the pages and their stories that they shared with me in 2C. I thank them, even though I may never see them again or don't remember by name. And they more than likely don't remember me.

The stories from the passengers in 2A can and probably do relate to many of the readers, and you may think you are the person I'm writing about. But more than likely I am not. We need to remember that we are all connected to one another, and our life situations are not too different from any others. We can all learn and grow from each other's life stories. In the end, I think that is my purpose for writing this book—to share conversations about topics that seem to matter to us all.

THANK YOU

I truly hope you enjoyed reading my stories and will spread the word about the book. We all have a story, and that's what our lives add up to when they're all done. I hope you are creating good stories in your life.

A good friend of mine once said, "There are three things in life that you can't get back: a thrown object, a spoken word, and a missed opportunity." I often remember this as I am driving down the road. I ask myself whether I've missed out on any good opportunities or spoken words that I would like to get back. As for the thrown objects, yes, I have probably thrown a few things that I would have been better off not throwing.

Tomorrow is another opportunity for us to be the people we should be and have the lives that we want. All we have to do is commit to change and then have the physical and moral courage to see it through.

I wish for life to bring you the best it has to offer. And when it does, don't forget to give back.

So safe travels and keep talking. Maybe my next edition will include your story.

ABOUT THE AUTHOR

Ken Cauthen grew up in Heath Springs, South Carolina. He left for the army when he was eighteen. He served for twenty years. During this time, he traveled and served in many countries, and he had opportunities to meet and talk with many passengers in 2A. He is now retired from service and lives in Florida. He still enjoys traveling and meeting new and interesting people. *Excuse me, I'm in 2A* is his first book

Excuseme.imin2a@yahoo.com

www.ingramcontent.com/pod-product-compliance
Lightning Source LLC
Chambersburg PA
CBHW031409040426
42444CB00005B/484